Retro Revamp

FUNky Projects, from HandBags to HouseWareS

bY Jennifer Knapp

pHotograPHs by Teresa Domka

iLLustrations by Jennifer Knapp

CHRONICLE BOOKS

SAN FRANCISCO

Library of Congress Cataloging-in Publication Data

Knapp, Jennifer.
   Retro revamp : funky projects, from handbags to housewares / by Jennifer Knapp ;
  photography by Teresa Domka ; illustrations by Jennifer Knapp.
     p.   cm.
   ISBN 0-8118-2523-X (hc)
   1. Handicraft. 2. Recycling (Waste, etc.) I. Title.
  TT157.K524 2000
  745.5—dc21
                                      99-37297
                                          CIP

Manufactured in China.

Prop styling by Jennifer Knapp
Designed by Sara Schneider
The photographer wishes to thank Jennifer and Sara for making the project so much fun.

Distributed in Canada by Raincoast Books
8680 Cambie Street
Vancouver, British Columbia V6P 6M9

10 9 8 7 6 5 4 3 2 1

Chronicle Books
85 Second Street
San Francisco, California 94105

www.chroniclebooks.com

ACKNOWLEDGMENTS

Thanks to my grandmother Alice for teaching me that every surface should be decorated, to my parents for encouraging that sort of behavior, to Aaron for putting up with it, and to Astro for wearing embarrassing dog collars with flair.

And special thanks to everyone who put so much creative energy into this project; Leslie, Mikyla, Sara, Amy, Laura, E.J., Teresa, Judy, and all my thrifting pals.

TABLE OF CONTENTS

9 Introduction

13 Techniques

18 Materials

20 Tools

23 Things to Collect

VAGUELY VOGUE

27 Holly Golightly's Dream Bag

30 Bizarre Bustier

32 Chopstick-do

34 Gypsy Fortune Teller Skirt

36 Eiffel Tower Sac à Main

38 Zsa-Zsa Jewelry Box

41 Button Bracelet

42 Charming Bracelet

44 Safety-Pin Bracelet

46 Do-It-Yourself Necklace

DECADENT DÉCOR

49 Comfy T-Shirt Quilt

52 Tweety House

55 Murder-Mystery Boxes

57 Ticktock Clocks

58 Midnight Moon Nightlights

60 Mismatched-Metal Medicine Cabinet

63 Mad Hatter Teapot

66 Bottle Cap Frames

69 Cigar Box Shrine

72 Queen Victoria's Bug Collection

TRENDY TRIMMINGS

75 Car Carma: Dashboard Shrine

77 Happy Smiling Wallets

79 Voodoo Dolls

80 Message in a Bottle

83 Flower-Power Bike Basket

84 Mr. Potato Head Beach Bag

86 Pink Posie Envelopes

FIESTA FURNITURE

89 Mystery Date End Table

91 Divine Dresser

95 Coca-Cola End Table

97 Ugly Chair First Aid

SERENDIPITOUS STUFF

101 Kindergarten Cards

103 How Do I Love Thee Valentine

106 Zen Paper Bowls

109 Paper Star

113 Zany Zoo

117 Dapper Dog Collar

118 Mice Madness

120 Sarah Bernhardt Digit Décor

122 Sources

123 Art Supplies by Mail

123 Reading Material

INTRODUCTION

We've all seen them: Grannies crocheting up a storm of pom-pom—topped cozies for everything from the toaster to the TV. The guy down the street who decorated his house with hubcaps and toothpaste tubes. They are the last practitioners of a sadly vanishing urban folk art. Not that making things by hand is dead. On the contrary, the hardcore "crafting" set is cranking out pinecone-encrusted twig baskets and bead-bejeweled styrofoam balls. But unless you stick to rolling honeycomb candles with the nouveau home ec crowd, you are generally considered a little off. But, folk art involves more than wielding a glue gun with bravado. This art form, alive and well in other parts of the world, usually consists of an apprenticed or self-trained artist using mainly found and recycled materials and working within a cultural tradition handed down through the generations. We may have lost many of our artistic folk traditions in the horn-honking mayhem of today's cities. But whether in the cities or sprawling suburbia everyone has one major folk art ingredient: an abundance of found (or findable) material. The world is a dumping ground of found objects. Most people have their own personal pile of out-of-control junk. What to do with it all? Instead of throwing it out the window, take advantage of the rich mix-and-match cultures of North America and create your own urban folk art traditions.

You don't have to be as wacko as the hubcap guy down the street to create urban folk art. The following "recipes" outline some fun and creative items to start you off. The projects are not meant to be pieces of trained craftsmanship. Folk art's free and easy aesthetic makes it simple for everyone. The finished works are all the more charming if they are a little kooky and eclectic. Big, clunky, colorful stitches and globs of glue here and there add to the "conversation piece." You'll hopefully be labeled an eccentric and wow your friends and offend your Aunt Myrtle.

There are many reasons to utilize found and recycled materials rather than popping down to Craft-O-Rama. Gathering items is fun in and of itself and much cheaper than buying everything new. You can give new life to abandoned and ugly items. Make the world a better place by rescuing a chair from olive-green-plaid hell. Each item will bring its own history and personality to the piece. Of course, a new piece of fabric will work in your sewing project, but a seventies polyester shirt or a fifties floral apron will add a whole new dimension. Old items encourage creativity and inspire ideas. Recycled items are free and you prevent them from ending up in the already overflowing landfill. Look for stuff crammed in the closet or under the bed. Raid Granny's attic and Mom's basement. Find that coffee cup you never got around to gluing together. Now you don't have to!

The creative part of each project really lies in assembling the materials. Haunt thrift stores, garage sales, and junk shops. Sift through piles of cast-off ephemera and find a treasure trove of one-of-a-kind items. Gather knickknacks on your travels—from Graceland to Istanbul to the corner Vietnamese grocery—pebbles, bottle caps, old photographs, ticket stubs, broken toys.

The projects in this book call only for readily available items, with plenty of substitution suggestions as well. But these should only be taken as suggestions, as a jumping-off point for your imagination. If the recipe asks for bottle caps but you collect Chinese coins, by all means use those. Perhaps the recipe calls for a board game, but you have an exquisite paint-by-numbers *Last Supper;* that's even better!

Many of the recipes utilize traditional craft store mainstays—glitter, sequins, and plastic jewels—available at thrift stores, as well. Those found at a thrift store are probably older and more interesting. If you're a recycling fanatic, use aluminum foil, pop cans, and broken mirrors to lend a twinkle to your piece. Maybe you won't find all the ingredients on your first trip to the secondhand store, but you might find that fondue pot or record album you've been looking for. Your finished piece will be that much more interesting if you think of the "material gathering" as a creative process. (Of course, if you are a get-things-done type of person, all of these projects can be made from new materials. Just run down to the craft store, elbow the blue-haired ladies out of the way, and load up!)

The projects are simple once you have the "ingredients" assembled. (For more information on gathering materials see the Sources section of this book for ideas on secondhand scavenging and mail-order art supplies. You will also find suggestions for reading material on folk art and related subjects.) To avoid frustration, read through the Techniques section for detailed tips before starting. Don't put off a project because you hate to sand. Prep-o-phobics should just skip that step. Just slap the paint right over the dirt. It will probably work just fine. Besides, if it peels in a few years, no problem; you'll want a different color by then anyway. Even the sewing projects are easy. They call for only three different stitches, most of which you mastered long ago (if not, they're described in Techniques).

Fancy craft store gadgets are great, but most people don't have them lying around the house. A few handy-man tools are a smarter all-purpose investment. See the Materials section of this book for some that you'll find useful.

Folk art is more than its function. The more fun you have and the more thought you put in to each project, the greater the happiness that will shine through on each finished piece. Your absolutely unique artwork will speak volumes of its maker and of the world around you.

TECHNIQUES

PAINTING

With the right products, painting is simple and fun. The wilder the colors, the less a bad prep job will show! Water-based paints are best because of their easy cleanup and their less noxious fumes. See the Materials section of this book for suggestions. Invest in natural-bristle paintbrushes. They will make all paint jobs more pleasant. Sponge brushes are a good second choice, with cheap bristle brushes best consigned to the garbage can. Always put down newspaper or a reusable tarp before beginning a project. If you do drip paint where it doesn't belong, clean it up with water and a rag before it dries.

Experiment with staining rather than painting raw wood. Some common household items that will stain raw wood are: food coloring, fabric dye, grape juice, Kool-Aid and colorful hair dyes. These dyes can be thinned with water and applied with a sponge brush (they might stain a natural-bristle brush). Then seal the stain with a light varnish or a spray-on glaze.

PREPPING

Everyone hates prepping. No instant gratification here, although it can save time in the long run. In this book, about all that's expected is some cleanup and maybe a little sanding. Call me cooty paranoid, but I generally like to give found items a thorough cleaning anyway. Throw it in the wash or dishwasher. Clean it with a little soap and a rough kitchen pad. This works on most items. Larger items can be hosed off. Remove all dirt, cobwebs, loose paint, or varnish by spraying and scrubbing with a brush or kitchen pad and some soap. If you are cleaning wood furniture, let it dry thoroughly and then sand it with medium-grit sandpaper. If you do not have sandpaper, use coarse steel wool.

On sticky stuff, such as price tags and labels, that is not removable with soap, various solvents work well. Some spray-on window cleaners will work. Experiment on a small area with lighter fluid, nail polish remover, or Bestine. These are very toxic substances: Do not use them all at once or mix them in any way! Read the labels and be careful. Better yet, just leave the sticky stuff!

SEWING

Running Stitch This is the granddaddy of all sewing stitches. If you learned to sew for kindergarten projects, this is the stitch you probably used. The classic: Poke the needle through the top of the fabric to the bottom, then up through the bottom to the top. Make each stitch about a fourth of an inch long and a fourth of an inch apart. Soon you will have a lovely dotted line of stitches.

Whipstitch This stitch runs along the edge of the fabric and binds the edge. Stick the needle down through the top of the fabric and over the edge back to the top of the fabric. Now stick the needle back down through the top of the fabric again and pull. Thus, you will have formed a loop around the edge. This is a good stitch to use on a buttonhole. Space the stitches very close together so as to seal the raw edge of the fabric with the loops of thread.

Folk-Art Stitch This simple decorative stitch is a variation on the whipstitch and is also known as the blanket stitch. Begin by making one whipstitch. Now run the needle back through the loop along the edge (see diagram). Begin another whipstitch a fourth of an inch along the fabric. Before the loop is pulled tight to the edge, thread the needle through the loop. Pull tight. You will have a row of connected whipstitches. This is also a good stitch to use on pulled-out sweater necks.

CUTTING METAL

Remove can ends with a can opener and then use tin snips to shape the pieces. Pop cans are made of such a thin material that after removing the ends they can be cut with scissors or an X-acto knife. The main problem with cutting metal is cutting yourself! If you have leather or canvas work gloves, wear them. Mittens will not work! Metal can be very sneaky—a metal cut is just like a paper cut except that this wound will be bloody, gaping, and require stitches. The folk-art stitch is not recommended, by the way! Also keep in mind how the piece you are creating will be used. Where will it be used? Will people be handling it? Are all the metal edges safely surrounded by nails or bent under? These are all questions that need to be asked. Nothing puts a damper on a party like a guest having his or her finger cut off by a really cool looking chair—and you the embarrassed hostess! It's worse than burning the meatloaf.

DRYING

Hair dryers are very handy for the impatient crafter. Even if you don't have a bouffant to tend, pick one up anyway. They speed up the drying of white glue, matte medium, and some paints. Read the package of the material you want to dry. Don't get caught in the predicament of burning the house down trying to dry flammable materials!

GLUING

It is nice to have a flat surface for items to sit on safely while drying. Make sure the objects are clean and dry before you glue. White glue can be spread with a brush or a small square of cardboard. See the Materials section of this book for suggestions on glues, and read the labels carefully. Except for with white glue, drying shortcuts are not advised.

GROUT

One of these projects calls for grout, which can be purchased ready-mixed at a hardware store. It is a bit messy and has a mind of its own. Remember, once it dries it's not moving and it will stick to almost anything, so be careful! This is not the project to attempt on your prize fifties Formica dinette set. Before using grout, lay down plenty of newspaper and have towels and water ready to daub up any bits that escape.

LAMINATING

Some of the recipes call for laminating flat images at a copy shop. If this is not possible, art stores sell self-laminating products. Wide strips of clear packing tape also work. It may not be as smooth as laminating, but in some cases tape works better because it is more flexible.

DRAWING

Different solvents, such as nail polish remover, lighter fluid, and paint thinner, can work in strange ways on magazine images and color copies. Even if you are not an illustrator, you can create some interesting images. Experiment with this on projects that call for flat paper images. Be careful with all the toxic stuff! Read the directions.

CUTTING WOOD

Most lumberyards will cut wood to your pattern for a very small fee. Take advantage of this service, which means fewer tools and less mess for you!

MAKING HOLES IN METAL

For most of the projects, using a hammer and various nail widths works well. Bottle caps, tin cans, and thin sheet metal can be "drilled" in this way. However, a drill is sometimes necessary—if you are making holes in coins, for instance. Sometimes sheet-metal fabricators will drill holes for a small fee.

MATERIALS

Any good art supply store should have many different varieties of the materials mentioned here, plus plenty of advice on their use. I will mention some brand names in case you are buying from a catalog.

MATTE MEDIUM

Liquitex produces both a matte gel medium and a gloss gel medium, both of which are acrylic mediums that thin with water. Matte creates a smooth finish, whereas gloss is shiny. Both are excellent sealants that form a waterproof surface when dry.

PAINTS

Indoor latex works well for the furniture projects. It is available in a variety of finishes from paint stores. For painting on metal and plastic and about any other surface, try Liquitex "glossies" acrylic enamel or Deka acrylic enamel. If you use a different brand (there are many), just look for something that thins with water for ease of cleanup. In a pinch, for small areas, use colored nail polish!

GLUE

Just because you are making crafts doesn't mean you need a glue gun! Other glues, though perhaps less handy, work a lot better. Basic all-purpose white glue works well on paper, cloth, and even wood. You will also need a super-stick glue that works on all surfaces. Bond 527 multipurpose cement glue works extremely well. It is similar to epoxy but without the messy mixing. It bonds all surfaces: ceramic, glass, plastic, metal, etc.

PLASTICINE CLAY

There are a couple of brands—Fimo and Sculpey—of colorful malleable clay that can be baked hard in your home oven. Plasticine clay is a good material to use to create certain objects you can't find like the perfect Eiffel Tower topknot for a jewelry box. Choose from various colors or paint the clay with acrylic enamels after baking.

EMBROIDERY THREAD

The bright colors look festive and distract from messy stitches.

CRAYONS

Always handy, and now they come in neon and glitter!

SANDPAPER

For prepping furniture. Coarse steel wool can be used in a pinch.

READY-MADES

An extraordinary number of items are available premade, including table legs, tabletops, mini rag dolls, and birdhouses. Look for these items if you need to save time. They are available at hardware and craft stores.

OPTIONAL

Art tape, a high quality multipurpose white tape. Varnish, spray sealant or even clear nail polish.

TOOLS

A few simple tools can make any project a whiz. Hammers may seem daunting; the image of many difficult things that need fixing may loom before your eyes. But everyone should be self-sufficient and owning a hammer can be the first step. Besides, there's something very satisfying about going around and pounding on things. Everyone can do it, no special instructions necessary. Just avoid the dreaded Fred Flintstone thumb! While you're at the hardware store, here are some tools you might consider:

HAMMER
Choose a good quality one, big enough to get more than dainty jobs done right.

NAILS
Various sizes, including a few fat ones and many $5/8$-inch copper brads and upholstery tacks.

X-ACTO KNIFE
Or another brand of small utility knife with a box of extra blades.

PAINTBRUSHES
Good quality, natural bristle. Ask for advice on which would work best with the paint you are using. Don't buy the cheap ones! You'll curse wasting the ninety-nine cents with the first big wad of bristles it leaves in your new paint job. This is the place to spend some money. Just take good care of them and clean them well with mild hand soap and water.

NEEDLE
A large-eyed slim embroidery needle.

PLIERS
Needle-nose pliers are very handy on many projects.

TIN SNIPS
Necessary if you are cutting up tin cans, but pop cans can be cut with scissors.

SCISSORS
Get a good sharp pair that will last forever.

OPTIONAL
Tile cutters, sewing machine, drill, screwdriver.

THINGS TO COLLECT

Start boxes to organize your finds. Soon they'll be overflowing and you'll have plenty of cool things for your first project.

SOUVENIRS
Postcards, snowdomes, keychains.

BUTTONS
Buy that ugly polyester shirt if it's got great buttons; on second thought, save the polyester, too.

LINENS
Grandma's hankies, tablecloths, dish towels, and other fancy embroidered items. People used to do needlework as a pastime—imagine!

GAMES
Old board games, Chinese checkers, game pieces, mah-jongg tiles, Scrabble letters, dice, nudey playing cards.

PLASTIC
Fruit, flowers, toys, beads, jewels, hair clips.

BOOKS
Yearbooks, anatomy books with cool clear plastic overlays, books of verse, miniature books.

COSTUME JEWELRY
Rhinestone poodles, mod sixties flower brooches, princess tiaras.

METAL
Bottle caps, tin cans, and boxes.

CERAMICS
Old figurines, chipped dishes, salt-and-pepper shakers, souvenir dishes.

PAPER
Vintage postcards, valentines, dress patterns, stamps, photographs.

ODD ORNAMENTS
Fake fur, jiggle eyeballs, glitter, sequins, feather boas, beads.

NATURAL MATERIALS
Pebbles, flower petals, sea glass.

VISIT THE NEW OLD WORLD
If you are lucky enough to live in a culturally diverse area or in an area with a strong Old-World community, search the shops for interesting finds. For example: Indian forehead dots and deity postcards; Japanese kids' stationery, toys, and chopsticks; Chinese rice paper and newspapers; Italian candy wrappers and plastic Popes; Mexican oil cloth, *milagroes*, and skulls; French Eiffel Tower stuff, mini perfume bottles, and fancy packaging.

vaguely vogue

HOLLY GOLIGHTLY'S DREAM BAG

This cute little bag is perfect for a few small items: a couple of dollars and a lipstick. What more does one need, dah-ling? Colorful satin ribbons are woven together to create a unique "fabric." The more imaginative the combination of ribbon colors, the more interesting the result. Try contrasting as well as complementary colors, such as aqua, navy, hot pink, magenta, and bright orange. At the turn of the century, silk cigar bands and silk ties were woven in a similar fashion. Holly would have made her bag in Coco's favorite noncolors: classic black and white.

$4 \frac{1}{2}$ yards each of at least five colors of $\frac{3}{8}$-inch satin ribbon

$\frac{1}{2}$ yard fabric for the lining

Tape ($\frac{1}{2}$-inch masking or white art tape, see Materials)

Needle and thread

1 interesting button

Optional (but highly recommended): Fusible interfacing, available at fabric stores. An iron will be necessary if interfacing is used.

A sewing machine is also handy.

1. Measuring and cutting each length of ribbon as you work, begin to lay out 15-inch-long strips of ribbon (alternating colors as desired) in vertical strips on a flat surface. Tape the top of each ribbon to the surface as you work to hold the ribbon in place. Make sure there are no gaps between the strips of ribbon. Stop when the ribbons measure $12 \frac{1}{2}$ inches horizontally.

2. Next, weave 12 $\frac{1}{2}$ -inch lengths of ribbon across the vertical strands in an over-and-under pattern, just like you would a lattice crust for a pie. Again, make sure there are no gaps between the horizontal ribbons, and tape the sides as you weave so that all the ribbon stays tightly in place. The end result will resemble a checkerboard that measures 15 x 12 $\frac{1}{2}$ inches.

3. To make things easy on yourself, fusible interfacing can be ironed to the woven ribbon "fabric" (follow the package directions). When ironed onto the wrong side of the ribbon, the interfacing fuses to the ribbon, sealing the strips in place.

4. Pin an enlarged version of the pattern to the ribbon and cut. Then cut out the same pattern on your lining material. If you do not use interfacing, tape the ribbon edges as you cut the woven ribbon according to the pattern.

5. Sew the two sides of the ribbon material together, right sides facing, and then along the base, leaving the "top" open, with a running stitch (see Techniques) or a machine. (If you are not using fusible interfacing, sew through the tape and then carefully remove the tape later.) Repeat this procedure with the lining material, again right sides facing.

6. Turn the ribbon pouch right side out and put the lining into the ribbon pouch.

7. Fold in about half an inch of both pieces of fabric around the top. With a visible running stitch neatly attach the lining to the ribbon pouch. As you

stitch add a 9-inch length of ribbon to each side for handles. Slip a half an inch of each end of the ribbon between the lining and the ribbon pouch to form a loop handle, and continue stitching to attach. Add a 4-inch length of ribbon in a similar loop to one side, centered, for the button closure.

8. Stitch on the button. A piece of old costume jewelry would also work well.

VARIATION: **If you don't have time to bother with weaving ribbons, stitch a bag out of faux fur (with perhaps a plastic daisy closure) or mod vinyl. Make one for every day of the week!**

Now off you go to a well-deserved breakfast at Tiffany's.

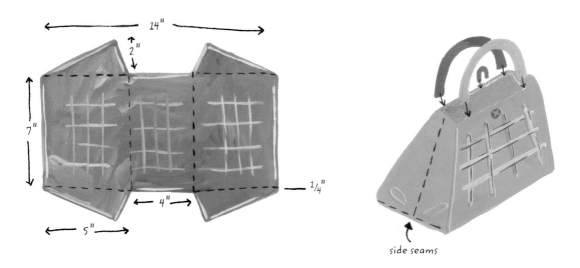

side seams

BIZARRE BUSTIER

Find a vintage bustier from the fifties (the really structured "girdlesque" ones with torpedo cups work best). By decorating with buttons, patches, and mini rosebuds, you can wear your underwear on the outside.

1 vintage or new bustier
1 package Rit dye (black is classic but any color works)
Needle and thread
Collection of buttons or flower patches or little silk rosebuds or bows
Optional: 3 yards flower-embroidered ribbon, velvet ribbon, or rik-rak,
    sewing machine

1. Many vintage garments come in a horrendous "nude" color that could better be described as "corpse." This noncolor must go! Dye your garment according to the dye package directions. Having the piece professionally dyed is an expensive but more durable option. Some fabrics will also refuse to accept anything but the most noxious professional dyes.

2. If you wish, sew a border of embroidered ribbon, rik-rak, or velvet ribbon around the top and bottom of the garment using a running stitch or a sewing machine. Adjust the shoulder straps to fit your body. Then sew the border material along each strap. You can even sew the border material under the garment cups and in vertical rows for that Parisian lingerie look.

3. Now sew buttons and/or flower patches and bows all over the surface of the garment. For the best durability, each item should be tied off individually.

   VARIATION: Entirely cover the garment with bottle caps to prove you are the queen of recycling. Drive a nail hole through each cap and sew onto the garment with embroidery thread. Dip rubber stamps in fabric paint and stamp the garment for a different decorative approach.

   Now you can walk around in your underwear without being arrested!

CHOPSTICK-DO

Do up your do in exotic style and add a bit of wow to your look. These hair sticks can be made in a minute for a terrific Top Ramen topknot.

Hammer

Two ⁵/₈-inch copper nails

1 pair children's wooden chopsticks. A regular pair will work but they just aren't the same without the wacky colors and kitty cartoon characters. Plastic are okay but will require a drill.

Multipurpose cement glue

2 plastic barrettes. Bows, butterflies, or airplanes, your choice.

Optional: Drill—if you are using plastic chopsticks you will have to drill a hole for the nails. Then glue the nails in place with the multipurpose cement glue. Rubber band or tape, plastic jewels, glitter.

1. Hammer a nail into the top of one chopstick carefully so as not to split the wood. If the wood splits, stop hammering and try drilling the hole instead. If you don't have a drill forge ahead and use your glue to glue the nail in and any split pieces back together. Place a rubber band or tape tightly around the outside to hold the chopstick together. After a few minutes, when the glue is set, carefully remove the rubber band or tape.

2. Clip a barrette around the nail and glue the barrette closed.

3. If you're really feeling crafty, glue plastic jewels and glitter to the barrette.

GYPSY FORTUNE TELLER SKIRT

Make some extra money on the side as a palm reader. "I see a tall dark stranger entering your life" and "I see good fortune in your future. For five bucks I can tell you more" are lines you will need to know. You will also have to look authentic. By decorating an existing skirt, it's simple to look like a colorful eccentric without being a seamstress as well. Old cotton fabrics from the thirties, forties, and fifties are perfect. Prints or plain colors, just make sure the skirt fits around the waist. Flowing peasant style is the most convincing.

1 secondhand skirt
Rik-rak, ribbon, flower-embroidered ribbon, quite a few yards and
    colors of each (the width of your skirt will dictate the length
    necessary)
Needle and thread or a sewing machine
Optional: Faux fur, flower patches, little silk flowers, bows, buttons.

1. Cut the skirt to the length you desire, then hem it by folding the cut edge twice toward the inside of the skirt and stitching the hem on a sewing machine or by hand using a running stitch.

2. Add a faux-fur pocket if you wish. First cut out a simple square of faux fur, then sew it onto the skirt.

3. Sew lengths of rik-rak and ribbon around the bottom edge of the skirt, one row on top of the other.

4. Sew a row of flower patches, silk flowers, or bows above the rik-rak.

5. Sew at least a dozen rows of decoration around the bottom of the skirt and two or three around the waist. Leave the center plain, or dot it with a field of fabric rosebuds.

   If you cut off the skirt and hemmed it, the fabric that made up the original hem can be sewn along the bottom of the skirt as a narrow, unobtrusive ruffle—no big square-dancing ruffles here! Or another former skirt hem could be used for a contrasting color.

   Now pull out your mysterious gypsy music and stare into your crystal ball.

EIFFEL TOWER SAC À MAIN

Sac à Main? That's French for purse! Look like you're sashaying down the Champs Elysées everyday even if you're in Cleveland. This sequined Eiffel Tower tote is easy to make; all you have to do is supply the poodle. Oui, oui, mademoiselle!

$\frac{1}{2}$ yard pink sequined fabric
$\frac{1}{4}$ yard silver sequined fabric
Needle and thread
2–3 yards black sequined ribbon
$\frac{1}{2}$ yard lining material
Optional: Zipper.

1. Cut four triangles of the pink fabric according to the pattern.

2. Strip the sequins off the edge of the fabric, so that you have about a fourth of an inch of plain fabric on all edges.

3. Cut four half circles and one square of silver fabric according to the pattern. Strip a fourth of an inch of sequins off the edges of the square. Sew the half circles to the large end of the pink triangles using a running stitch (see diagram).

4. Sew the black sequined ribbon around the edges of the four pink triangles and then crisscross to simulate the tower armature.

5. Sew the sides of the pieces together, right sides facing, leaving one side open. Use a running stitch.

6. Stitch the base of each pink triangle around the edges of the silver square.

7. Cut out a lining using the same pattern and stitch together on the wrong side.

8. Tuck the lining into the exterior sequinned fabric. Fold under about a half an inch of the raw edge on the sequinned and the lining fabric and stitch with a visible but neat running stitch around the opening. This would be the perfect opportunity to put in a zipper if you are talented in that way. Whether simply stitching or showing off your skills with a zipper, don't forget to add handles. Cut two 9-inch lengths of black sequined ribbon. Tuck a half an inch of the ends of each ribbon between the sequined fabric and the lining to form a loop on either side of the opening. *Voilà!*

side pattern

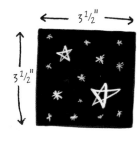

bottom pattern

trim piece for side

ZSA-ZSA JEWELRY BOX

Find a classic girl's jewelry box, with a ballerina inside. Revamp the outside with *East Indian* postcards, views of Paris, vintage *Vogue* magazine pictures, or even fur. Finish with costume jewelry, plastic jewels, and little mirrors. You can make a handle out of a perfume bottle, or an Eiffel Tower souvenir. Deck out the ballerina inside according to your theme whether it's with veils and a belly-dancing outfit or a mini Versace.

White glue
5 or more flat images (color copies, originals, postcards, or fabric)
1 jewelry box
Matte medium
$\frac{1}{2}$-inch-wide paintbrush
Plastic jewels, mirrors, costume jewelry, faux fur, glitter, paint, etc.
Multipurpose cement glue

1. With white glue, attach your images to the sides and top of the jewelry box. Let the glue dry.

2. Seal the images by brushing the entire box with matte medium. If you do not have matte medium, brush over the images with slightly watered down glue. This will not, unlike the matte medium, be waterproof.

3. Glue plastic jewels and mirrors and other treasures around the edges of the jewelry box. Attach the handle to the top of the box with cement glue. Decorate the ballerina with paint, faux fur, fabric scraps, and glitter.

BUTTON BRACELET

Instead of having your buttons all tucked away in your sewing basket or, worse yet, in various drawers along with paper clips and string (horrors!), make an old-fashioned button bracelet and enjoy their colorful simplicity every day. Then if you lose a button on your shirt, you'll have a new one right on your wrist.

6 inches black elastic $^1/_2$ inch wide or wider

25–50 buttons (depending on the size of your wrist and the size
    of the buttons)

Needle and black thread

1. Measure your wrist, adding an inch for overlap, and cut the elastic to size. Sew the ends of the elastic together by overlapping one side with the other by about half an inch.

2. Sew the buttons to the band, knotting the thread on the inside of the band. Tie off each button individually so the elastic will still be able to stretch.

3. Entirely encrust the band with buttons so that no elastic is visible.

VARIATION: Another way to make a button bracelet is to use only flat two-hole or four-hole buttons. Simply string a thin elastic thread through the holes on one side and then string another length of elastic thread through the holes on the other side. String enough buttons to fit around your wrist. String them tightly so they look like flat beads when you are done.

CHARMING BRACELET

Everybody used to have a charm bracelet on which to collect their favorite little mementos. Although the charms can't be found at every roadside attraction these days, charm bracelets can still be made from fun everyday objects or your favorite collection of seashells, bottle caps, plastic toys, Mexican *milagroes*, buttons, laminated images, photos, or other small items.

1 clasp

1 sturdy chain long enough to fit loosely around your wrist (available at bead shops and jewelry supply stores)

Needle-nose pliers

Collection of small charms, beads, *milagroes*, plastic toys, bottle caps with or without pictures (see Bottle Cap Frame for details), laminated photos of all your pals

Jump rings (small rings for attaching charms) and head pins (These resemble long pins without the point, and are used to attach items such as beads, with long narrow holes. They come in a variety of thicknesses; the thinnest are best.) Both items are available at bead shops and jewelry supply stores

Optional: Drill, or hammer and one thin nail.

1. Attach the clasp to your chain and make sure the bracelet fits around your wrist. It should be loose enough to accommodate the charms but not so loose that it falls off. If the chain is too big cut it with the pliers. All pliers have a cutting surface right next to the hinge. Add or remove links as necessary.

2. Attach an object to each link using whichever attachment (jump rings or head pins) seems to work best. Use the head pin for beads and other things with awkwardly placed holes. Slip the head pin through the bead. If the head slips through the hole, use a smaller bead first and then a larger bead. Now place the wire with the bead or beads through a link on the bracelet. Bend the wire back to meet the bead and wrap the wire end in a spiral around itself above the bead. Needle-nose pliers are handy for getting a tight wrap.

3. If the object you're attaching is already designed to be a charm and has a loop attached, so much the better! Simply secure the charm to the bracelet using a jump ring. Open the jump ring with pliers, thread it onto the charm and the bracelet link, then close the ring with pliers.

4. If you have something without a hole, you will need to make one. Bottle caps, seashells, and some toys will need holes. If you have a drill, get a very, very small bit and drill nice clean holes in each piece. The low-rent version of this is a hammer and a thin nail. Seashells will generally not survive this method, but it's worth a try!

5. If you are using laminated images, have the copy shop use the thickest plastic they have. Cut the image out, punch a hole in it with a large needle, and attach the image to the chain with a jump ring.

6. Continue this process until every link or at least every other link has an item attached.

SAFETY-PIN BRACELET

This is a good project if you're baby-sitting your niece for the afternoon. Simply clip beads onto safety pins and then string them together for a colorful cuff bracelet.

40–50 one-inch safety pins (the number will depend on the size of the wrist)

200–300 medium-size beads with a hole large enough to fit on a safety pin

1/2 yard black elastic thread

1. Open a safety pin and thread a few beads onto the open end. Close the pin. Beads that are all the same size work best but are not necessarily the most interesting. Take a safety pin with you to the bead store to find beads that will fit. Don't forget to try and close the pin as well.

2. After you have finished threading about forty pins with beads, lay the beaded pins out on a table and order them according to color and whim.

3. Alternate the pins so that the first one has its clasp up, the next has its clasp down, and so on. All the beads need to be facing up.

4. Now string a length of elastic thread through one side of the pins placing a bead between each pin—through a clasp, a bead, and then a bottom spring, etc. Then string an elastic through the other side including a bead between each pin.

5. Tie the two ends of elastic loosely. Fit the bracelet around your wrist and make the necessary adjustments for it to fit. You may need to add or subtract pins. It should have a snug, cufflike fit. Tighten the elastic and tie it into a knot. Trim the elastic ends.

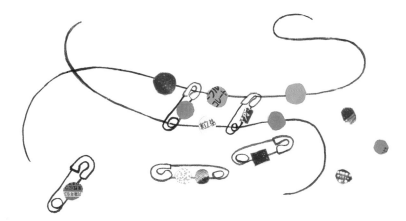

DO-IT-YOURSELF NECKLACE

This is a nice and inexpensive gift for a crafty friend. Hunt around for an old ink bottle, or any other short, squat little bottle or jar with a nice big opening. Many of the oldest are made from an opalescent glass that looks great when filled with colorful beads. Include beads, string, and a clasp to create a necklace project in a bottle.

Enough beads for a necklace or to fill the bottle
1 bottle or very small jar (an old ink bottle is best, but mini jam jars, often included in gift baskets, also work well)
Beading string (some string comes with a handy wire needle attached)
1 necklace clasp
1 cork or stopper
Optional: Beading needle, multipurpose cement glue.

1. Take some time collecting the beads—a few beautiful, more expensive beads with smaller seed beads, perhaps. Or maybe a couple of large beads and a leather thong instead of beading string. Whatever your whim.

2. Pour the beads into the bottle. Rattle the bottle around a bit to distribute the beads. Put the string and the necklace clasp on top of the beads. Stick a beading needle through the center of the beads if you wish.

3. Seal the top of the bottle with a cork whittled to size or a lid if you're using a jar that came with one. Glue a large bead to the stopper if you wish.

Decadent décor

COMFY T-SHIRT QUILT

If you have more T-shirts than days in the year in which to wear them, making a quilt from your favorites will let you enjoy your collection every day. Create mismatched mayhem or choose a theme: your soccer teams from grade school or your too-worn-out-to-wear concert tees. Another option is to make your own T-shirts by having your favorite images—vintage postcards, paint-by-numbers, Liberace album covers—made into iron-ons (see page 51 for details.) The possibilities are endless. Pick something cuddly. Maybe you find Japanese movie monsters really snuggly. Or maybe you'd prefer those large-eyed sixties Keane kids, staring and staring at you all night. Are they cute or depressing? This recipe makes a small, comfy, reading-a-book-on-the-couch quilt. But if you have T-shirts falling out of your closet, go ahead and expand it to double- or triple-bed size.

12 T-shirts or iron-ons on T-shirt material
1 flannel or jersey sheet, twin size, or a 36-inch x 72-inch length of
    flannel fabric
Needle and thread
Flannel backing fabric, 68 x 72 inches
Quilt bunting (an old blanket, twin size or bigger, can be substituted)
2 yards yarn
Optional: Sewing machine.

1. Cut the T-shirts into 12-inch x 12-inch squares, centering the image in each panel. Make a paper pattern for easy cutting.

2. Cut the twin sheet or flannel fabric into nine 4-inch x 12-inch strips, two 4-inch x 60-inch strips, two 6-inch x 56-inch strips, and two 6-inch x 60-inch strips.

3. Stitch together the images for the front of the quilt first by stitching a 4-inch x 12-inch strip of the sheet to the bottom of all but three of the T-shirt panels, using a running stitch, right sides facing or a sewing machine. Then sew four T-shirt panels together vertically, with one of the panels without the sheet at the bottom. Repeat twice.

4. Now you should have three vertical sections of pieced-together T-shirt panels with a strip of fabric between each image. Stitch these rows together vertically, adding a 60-inch x 4-inch strip of flannel between each section.

5. Next, frame the front panel of stitched-together tees with longer lengths of fabric, 56 x 6 inches on the top and bottom and 60 x 6 inches on the sides.

6. Then stitch, right sides facing, any three sides of the front panel to a piece of flannel backing cut to size, 68 x 72 inches.

7. Turn the quilt right side out, and fill it with bunting or a blanket, cut to size.

8. Stitch the open end of the quilt using a running stitch or a sewing machine with a matching color thread folding inside a half an inch of the front and back panels as you sew.

9. Sew 2-inch lengths of yarn through all three layers of fabric, from the front panel through the bunting to the back panel and then back up again to the top. Knot the yarn on the front of the quilt. Place the yarn ties every few inches to hold the bunting in place.

Now snuggle under your new old quilt with a flashlight and a good book. For cleaning, wash the quilt in cold water and hang it to dry.

OPTIONS FOR MAKING YOUR OWN T-SHIRTS: Have iron-ons made at a copy shop or even buy special iron-on paper for your computer. Follow the package directions for transfer carefully. Copy shops sometimes have machines for transferring, which will have better longevity than using a home iron. Follow all instructions for washing to also increase the iron-on's life span. Art supply stores have kits for silk screening fabric. Silk screening is much more involved, a project unto itself, but you will be rewarded with great-looking and long-lasting images. Another option is to make crayon shirts. Color a sheet of paper with crayons. Use a lot of pressure so the crayon wax is very thick on the page. Place the paper face-down on a T-shirt or jersey material, cover with a cloth, and iron using medium heat. The crayon will melt onto the T-shirt.

TWEETY HOUSE

Remodel little Tweeter's abode with a fresh coat of paint, some plastic friends, and a welcome mat. He'll be so happy with his new mansion he'll sing you sweet songs all day.

1 old or new prefab birdhouse (You can also look for old plastic dollhouses, such as Fisher-Price carrying case–style houses, barns, and airports, etc. Although these are getting expensive, the ones that have been left out in the mud and rain are reasonable.)

Paint, waterproof acrylic enamels are best (see Materials)

Paintbrush

Multipurpose cement glue

1 plastic bird

Optional: Pictures of birds, varnish or clear nail polish, plastic jewels, fake flowers, one small piece of Astroturf, and white glue.

1. If you have a building that is something other than an official birdhouse, you may need to remove the doors. Remember, birds do not know how to use door handles. But as long as the birds can get inside, your house will work. The entrance, despite popular opinion to the contrary, does not have to be round.

2. Give your house a new coat of paint. Contrasting colors on the roof and house are always stylish in Tweetyville. Or leave it as is. Let the paint dry.

3. If you have a way with the brush, you may want to add some bird and

flower paintings to the sides and top. If not, with white glue you can attach some bird cutouts to the house. Let the glue dry and then put a coat of varnish or clear nail polish on the cutouts to weatherize them.

4. Continue your decorative dalliance by gluing on plastic jewels and an Astroturf welcome mat if there is space. Glue a plastic bird friend to the top.

If your feathered friends are a little daunted by the grandeur of their new pad, sprinkle a bit of birdseed on the inside.

MURDER-MYSTERY BOXES

Searching for the materials is the fun part of this project. Before starting, you must find an old pulp-fiction paperback with a really great cover. Romance, detective, and sci-fi from the thirties, forties, and fifties are some of the best. Look for aliens invading earth or a woman in stilettos screaming into the phone. Your favorite find will create this handy little box that looks like a closed book.

1 pulp-fiction paperback
White glue
1 ready-made box (a wooden box, a cigar box, or even a cardboard
   box) close to the size of your book
Matte or gloss medium
4 large beads (for the feet), any shape but all the same size
Multipurpose cement glue
An interesting handle for the top: a large bead, a plastic alien,
   something you've sculpted from plasticine clay (see Materials),
   costume jewelry, a ceramic figurine, etc.

1. Using sharp scissors, cut the cover and the back off the book close to the spine. If this is too painful and you want to preserve the book, make a color copy of the front and back covers.

2. Squeeze white glue over the top surface of the ready-made box and spread the glue evenly to the edges. Attach the book cover to the top of the box. Attach the back cover of the book to the bottom in the same way.

3. Rip four text pages of the book into small 1-inch x 1-inch pieces. (If you don't want to miss all the intrigue and want to read the book, newsprint can be substituted.)

4. Spread white glue over the side surfaces of the box. Arrange the text scraps on the sides of the box so that they overlap (like a collage) with the lines of text skewed at various angles. Cover the box sides with paper all the way to the edges, cutting off overhanging bits where necessary. Let the glue dry.

5. Brush over the entire box with matte or gloss medium. Matte medium will leave a natural finish while gloss will have a shiny finish; both are waterproof. Whatever your preference, both products are available at art supply stores. Let dry. If you do not have matte or gloss medium, the surface can be brushed with slightly watered-down white glue; this will not, however, be a waterproof surface.

6. Place your box upside down on a flat surface. Glue the four beads to the corners of the box bottom with a multipurpose cement glue. Be sure that the hole in the bead is perpendicular to the box. Let the glue dry.

7. Create an interesting handle for the top of the box in keeping with the theme of your book. A plastic alien or UFO works for a sci-fi adventure, and a metal game piece from Monopoly or Clue for a detective story. If an appropriate handle cannot be found, sculpt one from plasticine clay according to the package directions. Attach the handle with the cement glue. If the cover is unbelievably cool, omit the handle.

TICKTOCK CLOCKS

Clocks have an important function—they let us know we're never on time. Despite the foreboding messages, they are occasionally handy.

Ruler

1 flat clock backing (barbecue trays, souvenir trays, and
   old paint-by-number masterpieces work well)

Drill, or hammer and a nail

1 clock mechanism (find an old or new battery-operated one)

Multipurpose cement glue

2 clock hands (barbecue forks, silverware, doll arms, pencils, or
   paint brushes; they must be fairly light to function properly.)

1. After using a ruler to find the exact center of your clock backing, drill a hole (or use the hammer-and-nail method) there. Attach the clock mechanism to the backing by sticking the hand-holder through the hole and securing the mechanism with cement glue. Sometimes the mechanism will snap in place when the hands are attached.

2. Drill a hole in the end of each clock hand. Attach the hands to the face of the clock. Different mechanisms will have various types of attachments. If you are working with an old clock, study how it was put together before you take it apart. If you have a new mechanism, it will have instructions.

MIDNIGHT MOON NIGHTLIGHTS

Make sure you can navigate your nocturnal wanderings to the refrigerator and bathroom without breaking a leg. Let these little sentinels guide you through the dark obstacle course that is your house, around Fido's water bowl and over the skateboard. They are also helpful in keeping that monster-under-the-bed where it belongs.

1 slide made into a $2\frac{1}{2}$-inch x 3-inch transparency

6-inch x 5-inch sheet of thin copper, brass, or tin (a pop can or a tin can will work)

Tin snips or scissors, depending on the thickness of the metal

1 piece of scrap wood, a least 7 x 6 inches

Hammer and nail

Multipurpose cement glue

One nightlight

4 inches wire

Optional: Metal faux finishing product, glue gun.

1. Take your favorite slide to a photo shop and tell them you need it made into a $2\frac{1}{2}$-inch x 3-inch transparency. This may take a few days.

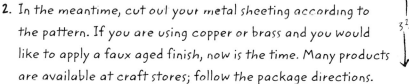

2. In the meantime, cut out your metal sheeting according to the pattern. If you are using copper or brass and you would like to apply a faux aged finish, now is the time. Many products are available at craft stores; follow the package directions.

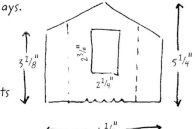

3. Lay your metal on a piece of scrap wood. With tin snips cut a hole in the center of the metal slightly smaller than the transparency. Do not worry about a perfect perpendicular cut. You could even make a wavy or zigzag border. Take the nail and pound zigzags, swirls, waves, stars, and crosses around the hole, much like is done with luminarias.

4. Frame the transparency in the metal sheet, attaching it with a glue gun or multipurpose cement glue by dabbing glue to each corner of the transparency and pressing it into the inside of the frame. Trim the transparency if necessary. Let the glue dry. Bend back the sides of the metal frame on either side of the transparency.

5. Remove the plastic shade from the nightlight. Make two holes with the hammer and nail in the metal frame below the transparency, one inch apart and half an inch from the bottom. String the wire through these holes, then wrap the wire tightly around the nightlight base below the bulb (there should be an indent of some sort from where the plastic shade fit). Plug in your new nightlight and turn it on to reveal the picture.

MISMATCHED-METAL MEDICINE CABINET

Old wooden medicine cabinets sometimes turn up at garage sales and flea markets. Commandeer one then cover your find with colorful pop cans, or for an industrial look use ribbed aluminum cans.

Leather work gloves
A bunch of old tin boxes, pop cans, olive oil tins, bottle caps, etc.
Can opener
Tin snips, or scissors if you are only using pop cans
1 wooden medicine cabinet or another small piece of wooden furniture
Hammer and $5/8$-inch copper nails

1. Don your work gloves and remove the tops and bottoms from the tins and pop cans with a can opener. Cut the tin or can along one side and then flatten it out. Cut various shapes (small squares, rectangles, flowers, curlicues, and crosses as well as various letters and words to create messages on your cabinet) from the pieces of metal with the tin snips.

2. Attach the shapes to the cabinet with a hammer and nails, pounding many nails along each shape's edge to cover sharp edges. Cover cabinet sides, the top, and frame the mirror or glass front.

3. Decorate the top further by nailing in more metal shapes so they stick up in a sort of tableau.

MAD HATTER TEAPOT

Although you see this method done almost to death on items at every trendy boutique, it is actually a very old tradition with a fancy French name to prove it. *piqué-assiette.* There is no better way to recycle your favorite pieces of sadly broken china. Add wacky figurines, cheap Chinese dishes, souvenir plates, Scrabble letters, beach glass, broken mirrors (change your bad luck to good), and plastic toys. Assembling the piece is a little harder than it looks. Take your time and work carefully with the grout so you end up with an *objet d'assiette* rather than a large blob.

1–2 pints grout, premixed and sand-free is easiest, but if you're really handy, mix your own

1 teapot or vase or other base object (the thrifts are full of ugly green florist vases; put one out of its misery)

Rag or sponge

A largish pile of broken ceramics and knickknacks

Optional: Tile cutter, hammer, zip-top bag, multipurpose cement glue, sandpaper.

1. If your ceramic pieces are of an even thickness (see step 6 if your pieces vary widely in thickness) apply grout evenly over one side of the teapot with your finger or a putty knife. Smooth with a damp rag or sponge.

2. Carefully stick the ceramic pieces to the grout one by one. If necessary break some of the pieces into smaller sizes to fill the gaps (see next page for details).

3. Continue until you have the entire surface covered with broken ceramic bits. Let the grout set for at least fifteen minutes. Repeat on the other side.

4. Once the pieces have dried firmly in place, smooth grout over the entire surface of your teapot. Make sure the grout fills the spaces between all the broken ceramics. With a damp rag, clean the grout from the ceramic pieces and smooth the grout between them. Let the grout set for fifteen minutes. Smooth a thin layer of grout over any cracked or rough spots. If your grout has become really uneven, let it set a bit longer and then sand it with medium-grit sandpaper. (This is a last resort; try to be careful when applying and smoothing the grout.) Now you know the difficult part! Follow the grout package instructions for set-up times.

5. Add "feet" to the teapot by coating the base with grout. Figurines, small buddhas, tiki salt-and-pepper shakers, and ceramic animals work well as feet. Next, carefully wrap a rope of grout around the connection point and mold it to the base grout like clay. Let the grout dry for 48 hours. If the feet still insist on falling off, teach them a lesson and affix them with multipurpose cement glue.

6. If you have ceramic pieces that vary in thickness by more than half an inch you may want to grout around and under each piece as follows: Apply a layer of grout to a small portion of the teapot, then stick on your ceramic piece. Roll a bit of grout between your fingers to create a rope. Wrap this "rope" along the edge of the ceramic piece. Continue in this method. Once

you have about a fourth of the base object covered, daub the grout with a damp rag or sponge using an up-and-down motion to even out the grout surface. Be sure to clean any grout off of the ceramic pieces with the damp rag.

7. If you need to break the pieces up, a professional tile cutter can be used for very exact cuts. But if you do not have a tile cutter available, place the piece in a zip-top plastic bag and use a hammer to break it. With some practice and a little care you can be quite accurate.

8. If you are using your fingers to mold the grout make sure to keep them rinsed and clean or use rubber gloves. Grout sticks to anything and everything!

Now you can enjoy that broken "I'd rather be thrift shopping" coffee mug you couldn't bear to throw out.

BOTTLE CAP FRAMES

Add some extra dimension to your photos with this multi-image frame. Bottle caps glued around the frame serve as mini frames for extra photos or found images. Display your pooch surrounded by shots of his unbearably cute snout, from every possible angle.

Small photos or images from magazines, color copies from books, etc.
Bottle caps, enough to cover the sides of the frame
Casting resin or clear nail polish
Multipurpose cement, or this would be the perfect opportunity to use
　　your much-maligned glue gun
1 picture frame, old or new (choose one with a flat front surface)
Optional: White glue, clear tape.

1. Cut your photos into small circles and fit them into the bottle caps. Secure them with a drop of white glue if you wish. Let the glue dry.

2. Pour in a dollop of casting resin to seal the photo, using the package instructions as a guide. This stuff is fairly toxic and foul smelling—it's what they used to create that glassy finish on those lovely seventies driftwood coffee tables. If this is all too daunting, use clear nail polish instead.

Although good and toxic in its own right, it comes in those friendly little bottles! Another option is glossy spray sealant, available at art supply stores. Some of your images may react badly to these products. Color copies are especially vulnerable to toxic meltdown. Test a small area first or seal the image with a layer of clear tape on the front and back.

3. Using cement glue, attach the bottle caps to the periphery of the frame. I hate to admit that a glue gun works well. However, multipurpose cement glue will be stronger. Place bottle caps on each corner of the frame first, then arrange more bottle caps between these corner caps. Fit as many as possible on each side of the frame.

CIGAR BOX SHRINE

A cigar box creates a ready-made space for a tabletop shrine. Not to worship cigars, silly, but for anyone or anything that needs a special place in your house. If you always lose your car keys and sunglasses maybe you need some help from St. Anthony, the patron saint of lost items. With so many saints and deities craving attention, put one of them to work for you.

1 cigar box
Blue, white, and black tempera paint
Paintbrushes (a $\frac{1}{2}$-inch-thick brush and a size 01 brush)
Buttons, sequins, or metallic pipe cleaners
Multipurpose cement glue
Plastic fruit and flowers, and other fitting decorative elements
Birthday candles
Tin snips
Tin cans
Hammer and nail
Scrap wood
Picture of your patron saint
1 flat Christmas ornament such as a star or a heart
Ribbon

1. Cut the cover from the cigar box with sharp scissors. Paint the interior of the box with the blue tempera. Let the paint dry.

2. Paint white clouds on the blue background. This is easy. Clouds are just a bunch of connected blobs so dip the big brush in white paint and then daub it up and down on the blue base. Let the paint dry.

3. With the small brush and the black paint, write a poem or a song across the sky background. You don't have to make this up! Just find something that fits with your theme. If this is too much work and you hate your penmanship, proceed directly to step 4!

4. Decorate the edge of the box along the top and sides with buttons or sequins or metallic pipe cleaners glued in place with multipurpose cement glue. The boxes are usually thick enough for buttons and beads to be glued along the edge.

5. Stand the box on end vertically. With multipurpose cement glue, attach the other decorations of plastic flowers, fruit, etc. to the bottom interior. A small dish from a child's tea set can also be glued to the bottom for offerings.

6. Glue a row of candles along the top exterior of the box.

7. With tin snips, carefully cut a triangle out of a can. The triangle's base should equal the width of the box top. Place the tin triangle on some scrap wood and use the hammer and nail to punch small holes through the surface. Make rows of holes to create star shapes and swirls, etc.

8. Glue this "pediment" to the back of the box, with the top of the tin triangle sticking up above the box.

9. Glue the image of your saint to a Christmas ornament. If a Christmas ornament is elusive at this time of year, cut a shape from a tin can. Attach a ribbon to the top of the ornament.

10. Glue the ribbon into the top of the box. Let the glue dry. The ornament should now dangle down into the interior of the box.

11. Complete the project with small shapes cut from a can, glitter, metal charms, and other ornamentation.

VARIATION: Instead of using a cigar box, create a mini shrine in a matchbox to carry along on your adventures.

— COUGH!

QUEEN VICTORIA'S BUG COLLECTION

If your collections are overflowing drawers, do what the Victorians did: arrange them neatly in a box and label them. The Victorians would wow their friends with assorted sad dead insects from faraway lands. If you haven't got any horned beetles, so much the better. Arrange seashells you collected last summer, beads you haven't strung, Barbie doll heads with various haircuts (a mohawk, a shag, and a mullet), or plastic bugs. Friends will be amazed by your flair at scientific organization.

1 cigar box
Black paint
Paintbrush
Vast collection of whatnots
Multipurpose cement glue
Pen and paper for labels
White glue

1. Paint the inside of the cigar box. Let dry.

2. Arrange your collection within the cigar box—by size, color, type, whatever works. When everything is just so, glue each item in place with multipurpose cement glue. Remember to leave room for labels. Let the glue dry.

3. Make a label for each item in your best shaky Victorian script. Cut out the labels and glue them under each item with white glue.

Trendy trimmings

CAR CARMA: DASHBOARD SHRINE

The place where one most needs a shrine is usually sadly lacking: the car. Whether you need a parking space or you don't want a flat, a personal patron saint is always handy. Choose a saint that gets the job done: Elvis, a sumo wrestler, Frida Kahlo, whoever can keep you out of a fender bender. Don't forget to make offerings of donut crumbs and spilled coffee.

1 corrugated cardboard box, any size
Various glues: White, multipurpose cement, even a glue gun
1 picture of a patron saint of your choosing
Appropriate saintly gear: jewels, birthday candles, feathers, candy
    hearts, plastic flowers, glitter, plastic figures, skulls, sequins,
    mirrors, metallic pipe cleaners, rik-rak, buddhas, milagroes, dice,
    shells, etc.
2 images related to your saint (i.e., Lotteria cards for Frida, Graceland
    for Elvis)

1. Cut a corner from the box, leaving a 4-inch x 3-inch section of the side and a 3-inch x 3-inch section along the bottom of the box with the corner as the joint between the two. With scissors round the corners on the base and cut a point in the back.

2. With white glue, attach your saint of choice to the back of the cardboard. Affix a saint-related image to the base of the shrine.

3. Wrap a metallic pipe cleaner around the edges of the box, gluing in place with multipurpose cement glue or a glue gun. The edges can also be decorated with glitter, rik-rak, or ribbon.

4. Now is the fun part. Cover your shrine with sequins, glitter, and plastic flowers. What shrine is complete without candles? Add a couple of birthday candles to either side. Continue to attach all of your decorations with multipurpose cement glue. Let the glue dry.

5. Don't forget the back of the shrine (the part that will sit against the windshield). Glue on another saint-related image with a few jewels so other drivers know not to mess with you!

beep

HAPPY SMILING WALLETS

Keep your friends' photos on the outside of your wallet rather than stuffed away inside! Laminate your favorite pics, greeting cards, and magazine clippings together. Whipstitch the edges with embroidery thread for a colorful smiley-face wallet.

White glue

Your favorite images: photos, kids' stationery, stickers, postcards, magazine clippings, illustrations, vintage dress patterns

1 sheet construction paper, $8\frac{1}{2}$ x 11 inches

1 skein embroidery thread

Embroidery needle

2 dots Velcro with self-adhesive backs

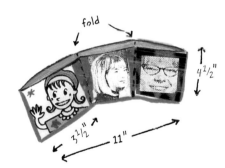

1. Using white glue, affix all of your images to one side of the construction paper.

2. Have this laminated with very thin plastic at a copy shop. Art supply stores have do-it-yourself sticky-sided plastic.

3. Fold the paper according to the diagram, with the images facing out. Whipstitch the two edges (see Techniques) with embroidery thread.

4. Attach the Velcro dots as indicated on the diagram for closures.

   Now fill your wallet with money. No wonder it's smiling!

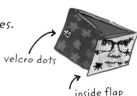

velcro dots

inside flap

VOODOO DOLLS

These dolls can bring good luck or bad. Encrust them with good-luck charms, fortune-cookie messages, and glitter for your friends. To torture your enemies, use bugs, locks of hair, and pins!

1 miniature rag doll, do-it-yourself or ready-made
Fabric paint, any color
Paintbrush
1 skein embroidery thread
Embroidery needle
1 key chain
Various beads, buttons, feathers, laminated photographs or sketches
   of friends or enemies, glitter, sequins, charms, pins, plastic bugs

1. Paint the doll using a color that represents the personality of the person you are depicting.

2. Create hair by cutting six 6-inch lengths of embroidery thread. Thread these lengths through the top of the doll's head, even out the ends, and tie a knot to hold each strand in place. Tie the key chain into the base of a center strand of hair.

3. Sew a laminated photo of your friend or enemy to the doll's face. Clear tape can be used instead of laminating. Cover the image with tape and cut around the edges. Decorate the doll with buttons, sequins, and glitter. For a more ominous version, use pins, plastic bugs, and eye of newt!

MESSAGE IN A BOTTLE

Instead of a boring old postcard, send a friend a little bottle full of souvenirs and a fortune cookie—style message from your vacation. Bottles can be filled with sand, beach glass, pineapple-topped toothpicks, and photo-booth pics from your trip to Florida. How about a ticket stub to the Empire State Building, a subway token, a plastic Statue of Liberty, and a wad of gum you found stuck to your shoe on your whirlwind tour of New York? These are also fun to keep on a shelf to remember all your trips.

1 small to medium-size bottle with a stopper
Collection of trinkets from your trip: rocks, sand, flowers, sea shells;
    coins from abroad; pictures, cut down to size, of you and, let's say,
    the Leaning Tower of Pisa; small toys, ticket stubs, beads,
    matchbooks, etc.
Handwritten messages
1 cork whittled down to size (if the bottle doesn't have a resealable
    cap)
1 label sticker
Optional: Candle wax, sealing wax.

1. Find a bottle. Old bottles look great and antique ink bottles have a nice large opening, but if you're assembling this during your vacation, you will need to be more practical. Check delis for mini-Evian, San Pelligrino, Martinelli's round apple juice bottles, or tiny Coke bottles, eight ounces or smaller, with clear glass.

2. Finding the trinkets is the creative part of this project. Assembly is a snap; just slip everything into the bottle, include a message about what a great time you're having.

3. Once everything is tucked inside, plug the opening with a cork. If you want a stronger seal, drip some candle or sealing wax over the top of the cork.

4. Label your trip on the outside of the bottle with a sticker, then package it up and mail it to your jealous friends. Or fill a shelf with your souvenir bottles, so on cold winter days you can look back wistfully at your "trip" to Acapulco.

FLOWER-POWER BIKE BASKET

Whether you have a cruiser, a Stingray, or a fancy titanium mountain bike, every bicyclist needs a festive flowered basket. Get rid of those ridiculous pockets under the seat and make something that can actually hold stuff. It's great for shopping—and you don't have to look like a mountain bike fanatic even if you are one.

Plastic or fabric flowers, plastic fruit, and other plastic ephemera
1 basket (plastic, wicker, or wire baskets are available at bike shops)
1 skein embroidery thread
Embroidery needle
Optional: 1 yard ball fringe, 1 yard rik-rak, multipurpose cement glue.

1. Decide how you would like the flowers to be arranged. Once you have an idea of your design, begin to stitch the items to the basket. First, cut the stems from the flowers with scissors. Use a large needle with the embroidery thread and tie off each item inside the basket. When making your stitches through the flowers, make sure your thread goes through each layer. Soft plastic can be stitched right through, but hard plastic will have to be stitched around or lashed to the basket.

2. You can finish the top rim of plastic baskets by sewing on a line of rik-rak. On wicker, this will need to be glued. If you would like ball fringe, sew it to the bottom edge of the basket so it dangles down happily.

MR. POTATO HEAD BEACH BAG

A big potato sack trimmed with festive Mexican tablecloth fabric makes the perfect tote for your vintage bikini. It's large enough to stuff in a beach blanket, your favorite book, and suntan oil. It's so big you can even fill it with groceries on your way home.

1 mesh potato or onion sack
½ yard vinyl tablecloth fabric (you may need more, depending on the size of your bag)
Embroidery thread and needle
1 foot nylon webbing

1. Cut off enough of the top of the sack so that you can carry it comfortably, without it dragging on the ground!

2. Fold your vinyl cloth horizontally along the bottom of the bag so that you have 6 inches of fabric on each side of the bag's bottom. Cut the vinyl with sharp scissors, leaving about an inch for a seam along the two sides of your bag.

3. Sew your vinyl, right side facing in, up both sides, leaving the top open. Turn the vinyl right side out.

4. Tuck your bag into the vinyl. This vinyl portion should cover the bottom of your bag and 6 inches up both sides. Sew the vinyl to your bag using embroidery thread and a whipstitch (see Techniques). Sew all the way around the bag with big decorative stitches. Be careful not to get so over excited about the beach that you sew the bag shut!

5. Cut the remaining vinyl lengthwise into 4-inch-wide strips. Wrap these vinyl strips over the raw end of the top of the bag so that you have 2 inches of vinyl on each side. Sew the vinyl in place using the same method as before. The number of strips you will need will depend on the size of your bag.

6. Cut the webbing in half. Singe the ends over a flame to keep them from unraveling. Sew the two pieces of webbing in place with embroidery thread for handles, one on each side of the bag and attached at their two endpoints, just like a tote bag. Be sure to sew the webbing through the top portion of vinyl as well as the mesh underneath to assure a sturdy handle. Make the loops longer if you want to be able to hook them over your shoulder.

PINK POSIE ENVELOPES

Talk your Grandmama out of a couple of her cute hankies. All covered with violets, posies, and forget-me-nots, these can be stitched into charming little envelopes in less than a minute. Really!

2 square hankies
1 skein embroidery thread
Embroidery needle
1 button

1. If the two hankies are not the same size, trim one to size. With the embroidery thread, stitch the hankies together around the outside edges using a decorative folk-art stitch or a whipstitch (see Techniques).

2. Fold three corners of the hanky to the center to resemble an envelope (see diagram). Stitch the two seams where the sides meet with a whipstitch or folk-art stitch.

3. Sew the button to the center of the three corners. Cut a hole in the flap of the hankies for the buttonhole. Whipstitch the edge of the buttonhole.

OPTIONAL: You can even make a stamp from a piece of fabric cut with pinking shears. Sew this to the plain side of your "envelope." Embroider the name of your intended recipient on it to make it even more envelopey.

Cute, cute, cute. So sweet you can almost smell the posies.

fiesta furniture

MYSTERY DATE END TABLE

Will he be a dream or a dud? Unfortunately, he'll probably stand you up! The Mystery Date game is almost impossible to find at thrift stores anymore, but there are tons of other fun games out there: Chinese checkers, Ouija boards, Clue, and Monopoly. Cover them with Plexiglas and they make great end tables. Better yet, they can still be played!

1 fun old board game
1 piece $^3/_4$-inch plywood, cut to the size of your game
Plexiglas, cut to the size of your game
Hammer and $^5/_8$-inch copper nails
4 ready-made table legs (see Materials) with attachments
Paint, latex interior or acrylic (see Materials)
Paintbrush
Mirror clips
Optional: Ball fringe, bird and butterfly pins, multipurpose cement glue.

1. Take your game to the lumberyard and have a piece of plywood cut to size. If you can find an end table that is the same size or slightly smaller than your game, then great, you're halfway done already!

2. Have a piece of Plexiglas cut to size also.

3. Nail the game to the plywood, hammering a nail into each corner of the game.

4. Attach the ready-made table legs according to the directions. Or drive screws though the plywood and into the legs *before* attaching the game.

5. Paint the legs and the $^3/_4$-inch edge of the plywood. Optional: ball fringe can be glued with multipurpose cement glue to finish the edge. Let the glue dry. If you can find them, nail little tin bird and butterfly pins to the table legs.

6. Attach the Plexiglas to the top of the game with mirror clips. Dig around at the hardware store for clips that when nailed to the side will overlap the Plexiglas and hold it in place. Nails can also be used. Or create your own clips from metal can lids, nailed to the side and then bent over the top of the Plexiglas.

DIVINE DRESSER

This decorative technique can be used to spruce up any piece of furniture. It's great for someone who is too lazy to refinish or for furniture that's so hideous that it's best to cover up as much of it as possible.

> 1 dresser
> Vinyl tablecloth fabric or paint-by-numbers artwork, or laminated
>   images (see Variations, below)
> Wood glue
> Leather work gloves
> Tin snips
> Sixty 3-inch-diameter tin can tops (the number will vary depending
>   on your dresser size)
> 6 pop cans
> Hammer and $^5/_8$-inch nails
> 50 bottle caps (the number will vary depending on your dresser size)
> Optional: Latex paint, paintbrush, sandpaper.

1. Remove any drawer pulls from the dresser. If necessary, lightly sand and paint the exterior.

2. Measure a side, the top, and one of the drawers of the dresser. You do not need to measure the back. Cut the vinyl according to these measurements: two sides, one top, and one for each drawer.

3. Spread wood glue evenly across the back of the vinyl pieces. Glue the vinyl

pieces to the wood, one to each side of the dresser, one to each drawer, and one to the top.

4. Don your work gloves. Using tin snips cut the tin can tops in half. Remove the tops and bottoms from the pop cans. Cut the pop cans along one side and then flatten them out. Cut flattened pop cans into 1-inch strips.

5. Nail the tin can tops around the perimeter of the vinyl panel on each drawer to form a scalloped border. The flat end of each can top should be flush with the edge of the drawer, with the rounded edge of the can top overlapping the vinyl. Can tops should overlap by about half an inch. Repeat this process on the top of the dresser.

6. Nail the bottle caps in place along the edge of the dresser top, color side up, driving a nail through the center of each cap. Cover the front three sides of the dresser's top edge. Nail the pop can strips around the edges of the two side panels of the dresser.

7. Reattach the drawer pulls. Find some cool old ones or make your own by pounding spoons, knives, or forks around a two-by-four to create pull-style handles, or by nailing bottle caps or metal buttons to wooden knobs.

OPTIONAL: Cut decorative shapes out of tin cans to nail, centered, in the vinyl panels. Replace the vinyl with paint-by-numbers artworks, album covers, or other images sealed with varnish or gloss medium. Replace the bottle caps with foreign coins or metal buttons and pins.

COCA-COLA END TABLE

For this project you may have to rummage around flea markets and dumpsters to find a partitioned wooden box such as an old soda-bottle box or a typographer's case. Fill the compartments with one of your many collections: fly-fishing lures, salt-and-pepper shakers, or plastic bugs. Cover the box with a piece of Plexiglas, attach some ready-made table legs, and tah-dah! An end table, display case, and storage unit all in one.

1 quart semigloss latex indoor paint and brush
Partitioned wooden box
Ready-made table legs with attachment hardware (usually included),
   available at hardware stores and lumberyards
Your favorite collection of small doodads
Multipurpose cement glue
1 sheet Plexiglas cut to fit the top of your box
Mirror clips
Optional: Hammer and nails; tin can; sandpaper; drill; screws and
   screwdriver.

1. Paint the inside of the box or leave it natural. If you're lucky it will have a cool pop logo on the outside. Of course a cleaning and light sanding will help the paint adhere, but do not put this project off because you hate prepping—painting over the cobwebs works almost as well!

2. Attach the ready-made table legs with the provided hardware according to

the directions. Or drive screws through the bottom of the box and into the tops of the legs with a drill and screwdriver. Don't use nails, as they will eventually loosen and leave you with a bad case of wobbly legs.

3. Paint the legs. Let the paint dry.

4. Attach your collection of doodads to the inside compartments of the box with super-strength multipurpose cement glue. Do this by laying the table on its side and gluing each object into a compartment. The object can be glued to the bottom or the side of the compartment, depending on the depth of each compartment and the size of the object. Don't forget that you will want to be able to see the object easily once the table is assembled. Let the glue dry.

5. Set the table upright and attach the Plexiglas with mirror clips to the top edge of the box.

VARIATION: If you do not have mirror clips, cut lengths of tin or aluminum from cans in 1-inch strips. Nail one edge to the side of the box and then pound around the edge so that it overlaps the Plexiglas to hold the top in place.

UGLY CHAIR FIRST AID

Sometimes the only secondhand chairs you can find are so ghastly you'd rather just sit on the floor. With a bit of paint, however, some of the ugliest can be rescued from the hell in which they are trapped. While you are searching for those perfect chrome and vinyl dream chairs for your dinette set, do a couple of less fortunate chairs a favor. Even those terrible bentwood ones can look, if not great, at least better.

Sandpaper

1 chair, wooden and structurally sound (if there is a missing seat you
     will need a piece of plywood cut to the size of the seat—beg them
     to cut it at a lumberyard, and bring a paper pattern)

Hammer and nails

Interior latex paint

Paintbrush

Upholstery foam, 1 inch thick at least

Upholstery material: vinyl, faux fur, patterned polyester, fancy brocade

Upholstery tacks

1. Lightly sand the chair. Nail the plywood seat to the chair if necessary. Paint the entire chair. Let the paint dry.

2. With scissors, cut your upholstery foam to the size of the seat. Place the cut foam on the upholstery material. Cut the fabric with an extra 3 inches all the way around. Place the foam on the chair seat. Place the upholstery fabric on top of the foam, tucking the ends of the fabric under the foam. Fold the fabric into pleats around the corners.

3. Hammer the upholstery tacks—evenly spaced about half an inch apart, or with no space—around the edge of the fabric. The tacks will cover about half an inch of the fabric edge and can go through the foam and into the wood of the chair seat. (If you are using thicker foam, simply pull the fabric out about half an inch and then nail through the fabric only.)

SeRenDiPitOus stuff

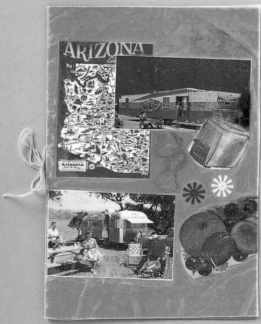

KINDERGARTEN CARDS

This old trick from kindergarten is still fun in your old age! Grated crayons, little photos, magazine clippings, fortune-cookie messages, glitter, and other flat things are all sandwiched between wax paper and then ironed. Add construction paper and you have cards for every occasion.

2 sheets wax paper, 1 foot long
2 pressing cloths or thin kitchen towels
Various flat objects: magazine and newspaper clippings, maps,
       flattened cocktail umbrellas, playing cards, stickers, fabric, leaves,
       and pressed flowers are just some of the many ideas.
X-acto knife
Crayons
Iron
1 piece construction paper, 9 x 12 inches
Embroidery thread, various colors
Embroidery needle

1. Place one sheet of wax paper on top of the pressing cloth or towel on an ironing surface.

2. Place your flat items face up on this sheet of wax paper. The images on the right half of the wax paper will be on the front of the card; the images on the left side will be on the back.

3. With the X-acto knife, grate some crayon around and over the images. Be fairly liberal; wax paper is not what it used to be, so the crayon wax will really help the card seal.

4. Place the second sheet of wax paper carefully over the top of the first sheet.

5. Cover both pieces of wax paper with a second pressing cloth or thin towel. Iron on medium heat.

6. Carefully peek under the cloth to see if the wax and crayon have melted and fused. If not, continue to iron. Let the paper cool.

7. Fold the wax paper in half, right side facing out. Fold the construction paper in half.

8. Slip the construction paper inside the wax paper. Sew the papers together by poking two holes in the spine and drawing the thread through. Then tie a bow on the outside of the card.

9. Trim the wax paper neatly around the edges to make it even with the construction paper.

HOW DO I LOVE THEE* VALENTINE

This is a super-romantic valentine to give anytime, and you don't even have to write one verse! Find an old book of ultra-gooey love poems. Visit the dusty, rarely seen poetry section of a used-books store and look for collections of Byron, Shelley, and Browning. Shakespeare's sonnets are another good choice for a literary honey-bunny. Paint and decorate the inside of the book with small hearts, personalized notes, photos, and even nudey playing cards! Highlight your favorite poems by decorating around their edges or, if you're really daring, write a rhyme of your own. "Your eyes are like roses, I adore your cute toeses" is always a good beginning.

1 old book of lovey-dovey poems. Small, 3-inch x 5-inch editions are
    the best. Just make sure you aren't mutilating a first edition!
Day-Glo feathers, glitter, and sequins
Crayons or paint
A collection of romantic tidbits: Photos of you and your Romeo or
    Juliet, antique valentines, kiddie valentines with envelopes,
    stickers, vixens from the fifties, ravishing red-lipstick kisses, etc.
White glue
Embroidery thread, various colors
Embroidery needle

1. Decorate the pages with drawings, glitter, and sequins. Highlight your favorite verses by drawing garlands of flowers around the edges.

2. Glue or sew photos, paper hearts, valentines, and other romantic images into the pages of the book. Cut heart shapes out of the center of some pages in the book to frame your photos.

3. Hand write messages, slip them into little envelopes, and glue the envelopes to the pages. Seal the envelopes with a lipstick kiss.

* "How do I love thee," was uttered, well, at least written down by Elizabeth Barrett Browning—so follow her example and become a hopeless romantic.

ZEN PAPER BOWLS

These beautiful and simple bowls can be molded from paper scraps, leaves, or flower petals and embedded with sequins, colored threads, and foil. Paper choices can include: rice paper, magazine clippings, wrapping paper, origami paper, postcards, pages from old books, sheet music, seed packets, and paper dolls. Even when made from crazy colorful comics, these bowls maintain a sort of detached calm. How? They are reincarnated Zen masters!

Paper scraps
1 ceramic or glass bowl to use as a mold
1 large plastic bag
$1\frac{1}{2}$-inch paintbrush
Matte medium
Optional: Hair dryer, needle-nose pliers, masking tape, 1 yard copper wire, dried and pressed leaves or petals (dry but bendable).

1. Tear your paper scraps into pieces that are approximately 1 x 1 inch.

2. Turn the bowl upside down on a flat work surface.

3. Cover the bowl with the plastic bag, tucking the excess plastic underneath. Use masking tape to secure the plastic if necessary. The plastic should fit snuggly but need not be smooth.

4. Begin to apply the paper scraps by holding a piece against the form and brushing it with the matte medium until the paper is permeated. This

application is just like papier-mâché. The matte medium can be thinned with water if it is too gloppy. Simply dip the brush in water before putting it in the matte medium.

5. Continue in this way with paper scraps and rose petals (if using) until the entire bowl is covered with one layer of paper.

6. Let the paper dry. This process can be sped up by using a hair dryer.

7. Carefully extract the ceramic bowl from underneath the molded paper, then slowly pull the plastic away from the interior of the paper bowl. The bowl is still quite thin at this point so take your time. Don't be too worried, though; any slight tear can be patched later.

8. Apply another layer of paper to the inside of the bowl using the same method as before. The number of layers you apply will depend on the thickness of your paper, but two to three total layers should be enough. Just make sure to let the paper dry between the layers.

OPTIONAL: To make "feet" for your bowl, cut 1 yard of copper wire into three 6-inch lengths. Make a flat curlicue out of each length by holding one end of the wire with needle-nose pliers and loosely wrapping all but 1 inch into a spiral. Hammer the spiral to flatten it if necessary. Fold the 1-inch straight portion of wire up and perpendicular to the spiral. Stick this section through the bottom of the bowl. Bend the prong projecting through

the inside of the bowl to hold the foot in place. The three feet should be positioned symmetrically around the base of the bowl. Layer a piece of paper with matte medium over the wires on the inside of the bowl to cover the ends. Let the paper dry. Set the bowl upright and bend the wire feet if necessary to make the bowl stand straight.

Now, on your next crazy, hectic, insane day, just look at this bowl to see how calm something can be. Then pitch it out the window in disgust. Not to worry; it's so relaxed it won't break!

PAPER STAR

When closed, these delicate stars resemble books. Untie the ribbon closure and they magically fan out into a star. For holidays or every day, a few simple folds create a complex-looking ornament.

> 1 sheet 22-inch x 30-inch paper (colored art paper works best; the
>   paper must be colored on both sides and fairly thick for durability)
> White glue
> Cardboard, 6 x 6 inches
> Wrapping paper or patterned paper or marbleized paper
> 14 inches ribbon
> Optional: Metallic pen.

1. Cut the colored art paper into four $2\frac{1}{4}$-inch x 30-inch strips.

2. Attach two strips of paper together by overlapping one end with the other by $2\frac{1}{4}$ inches and gluing the overlapped ends. Let the glue dry. Repeat with the remaining two strips of paper. You will then have two strips of paper measuring $2\frac{1}{4}$ x 58 inches.

3. If you wish, decorate both sides of the paper strips with the metallic pen. Draw stars and swirls or write a poem (not a great one, because some of the words will be obscured).

4. Cut two squares of the cardboard measuring $2\frac{1}{2}$ x $2\frac{1}{2}$ inches.

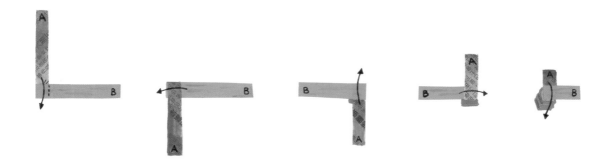

5. Cover one side of each cardboard square evenly with white glue.

6. Place the cardboard, glue side down, on the wrapping paper.

7. Cut the wrapping paper out around the cardboard, leaving a half-inch border.

8. Spread glue across the other side of the cardboard and wrap the half-inch of wrapping paper around the edge of the cardboard. Fold the wrapping paper around the corners of the cardboard as if you were wrapping a present. Hold the paper in place and let the glue dry.

9. Now it is time to fold the interior papers that will create the star. This is very simple: no complex origami! Take the two ends of your colored art paper strips. Overlap one with the other to form an acute-angled corner, (see diagram). Alternate folding the strips one over the other, creating a fold every $2\frac{1}{4}$ inches. This is an accordian fold done with two strips of paper rather than one, almost like a simple braid.

10. Continue folding to about 54 inches. Cut the excess paper to make it even with the folded paper.

11. Cut the ribbon into two 3-inch lengths and two 4-inch lengths.

12. Place the cardboard, covered side down, 1 inch apart on a flat surface. Glue the 3-inch lengths of ribbon between the two cardboard squares with ³/₄ of an inch between the two ribbons. One inch of ribbon will overlap each cardboard square, with 1 inch between the two squares. The ribbons will act as the hinges, or bookbinding, that will hold the two pieces of cardboard together. Let the glue dry.

13. Center the 4-inch lengths of ribbon, one on each cardboard square, on the opposite side of the hinge. These will tie the book closed. Glue the ribbon to the cardboard and let the glue dry.

14. Slip the folded art paper into the cardboard binding. Glue one end of the folded art paper to the cardboard "cover" and one end to the back. Tie the ribbon closure together and place a heavy book on top until the glue dries.

ZANY ZOO

Are they alligators or elephants or polka-dotted pooches? How about a combination of each. Pull out your old fabric scrap bag and hope that it is full of fuzzy fleece, fake fur, mod sixties flower-power polyester, and ball fringe. If it's not, time for a trip to your local thrift. The thrifts are always full of odd fabric bits and pieces, but also dig through their clothes for great prints and their stuffed animals for weird faux fur. The wilder the fabric combinations, the better the mismatched-menagerie look. Don't worry about symmetrical cuts or neat stitches, just have fun and be creative. Add a backpack and a miniature pet and your "eleroo" (a combination of an elephant and a kangaroo) is ready for an adventure.

An out-of-control pile of fabric scraps
3 skeins variously colored embroidery thread
Embroidery needle
Small plastic animals, ball fringe, buttons, bottle caps, plastic hair clips,
    sequins, patches, etc.
Straight pins
Optional: Polyfill or cotton balls.

1. Cut a shirt or dress out of a fabric scrap, freehand or with the pattern (see next page). Cut out fabric legs, freehand or with the pattern. Using a simple running stitch (described in Techniques) attach them to the shirt or dress. The colorful embroidery thread is meant to be visible.

2. Decorate the body to your heart's desire. Add a front pocket, rows of buttons to the arms and legs, bottle caps, small plastic toys, a heart in the right place, and fringe. Add appliqué hearts and flowers cut from contrasting fabric anywhere and everywhere.

3. Pin the decorated piece to a backing fabric and cut out the outline. Stitch the back to the front using embroidery thread and a decorative folk art stitch or a whipstitch (see Techniques.) Your stitches will be visible all along the edges. Leave an opening at the neck.

4. Stuff the body with polyfill, cotton balls, or bits of soft fabric.

5. Fashion a head according to the pattern. Or improvise by making a huge hippo head or an elephant snout. Stuff the head and attach it to the body with big, colorful, anything-goes stitches.

6. Add fabric ears and button eyes and even a hair clip. Decorate the back with more buttons and patches and add a fabric tail. Cut ears, tails, and other additions freehand.

Use inventive color combos and materials and don't worry if they look goofy, that's the point—a small friend will love them all the more. Remember, buttons and other small items are dangerous for very small children. Five and up is a safe bet, or perhaps a very level-headed four-year-old.

PATTERNS: Enlarge these patterns on a copy machine to the indicated sizes or use as a reference to create your own patterns.

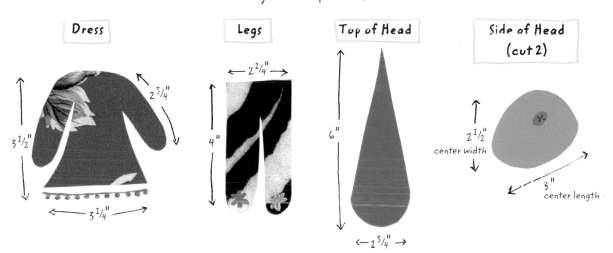

| Dress | Legs | Top of Head | Side of Head (cut 2) |

Dress: 3 1/2", 2 3/4", 3 1/4"

Legs: 2 1/4", 4"

Top of Head: 6", 1 3/4"

Side of Head: 2 1/2" center width, 3" center length

SEWING DIAGRAMS: Sew one side of the head to the top of the head using a folk art stitch (see diagram 1). The narrowest portion is the nose, the widest is the back of the head. Sew the other side to the top of the head in the same manner (see diagram 2). Finish the head by sewing the two sides together along the bottom (see diagram 3).

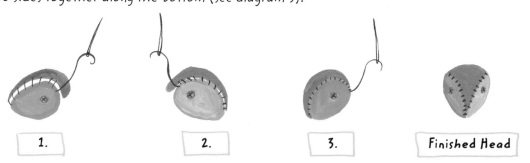

| 1. | 2. | 3. | Finished Head |

DAPPER DOG COLLAR

Now that everything in your house is encrusted with your eclectic thrift finds, your dog is going to look really plain! Every dog lover knows that dogs like nothing more than being dressed up in ridiculous costumes, especially if this includes a ride in a doll carriage. Well, with this project you can have your fun and not annoy your pooch quite as much.

5 inches faux fur (short fur works best)
1 dog collar, old, new, or make your own from webbing (available at fabric stores, along with closure clips)
Needle and thread
Multipurpose cement glue
Fabric flowers, fun patches, and plastic jewels
Letter beads
Optional: $1/2$-yard ball fringe

1. Cut the fur to the length of your collar, then fold it around the collar. Stitch a seam down the length of the collar just off the center. Stitch another seam the entire length just off the center on the other side, so you will have two rows of stitches for extra strength.

2. Glue the fabric flowers, patches, and jewels directly to the fur on the outside of the collar. Sew on the letter beads to spell out your pooch's name. Add ball fringe, if you wish, by stitching it to the inside, positioned to dangle jauntily from the bottom edge of the collar.

MICE MADNESS

Well, we can't let Fido have all the fun now can we? What would your cat love more than a catnip mouse? Okay, Ms. Know-It-All, maybe Fluffy would prefer a decapitated real rodent. But no one else in the house would!

* **Fabric scraps**
  1 skein embroidery thread
  Embroidery needle
  Polyfill or cotton balls
  1 foot yarn
  Catnip
  2 buttons

1. Create the body of your mouse by setting a glass on a piece of fabric and tracing around the glass. Cut out the circle and then cut it in half.

2. Sew the two halves of the circle together, right sides facing, along the rounded edge. Turn the fabric right side out and stuff the "body" with polyfill or cotton balls. Set the body, open side down, on fabric, trace, and cut out what will become the base of your mouse.

3. Stitch the base to the body with embroidery thread, using a folk-art or whipstitch (see Techniques). Before you stitch all the way around, sew in a piece of yarn for a tail and stuff in a little catnip. Cut a couple of ears out of the fabric, freehand, and stitch them onto the head. Sew on the buttons for eyes.

SARAH BERNHARDT DIGIT DÉCOR

Finger puppets can be created in a variety of ways for endless hours of entertainment. Act out your favorite sitcoms or make up a soap opera based on your real life. Discover your inner drama queen.

> Clay (see Materials)
> Beads, jewels, construction paper, colored electrical wire, and other fun bits
> Fabric scraps for outfits
> Needle and thread
> Multipurpose cement glue
> Optional: Acrylic paints, paintbrush.

1. Stick a blob of clay on your finger. Shape it into your favorite character: a princess, a wicked witch. If you are not a sculptor, simply pull out a nose and leave it at that. If you are absolutely hopeless, see the variation below.

2. Add beads for eyes, hairs in nose warts, jewel earrings, electrical wire to robots and Frankensteins, etc.

3. Let the clay dry or bake according to the package directions.

4. Paint the clay figure if you wish. Let the paint dry.

5. Take a small piece of fabric, about 2 x 3 1/2 inches. Wrap this loosely around your finger in a cone shape. Sew a seam parallel with your finger.

6. Drop a blob of glue into the finger hole of your puppet's head. Stick your fabric-clad finger into the hole, then carefully remove your finger. Let the glue dry.

7. Adorn your puppet with hats and crowns and other necessary costumes.

Now it's time to write your epic play!

VARIATION: Use old Barbie heads instead of clay. Paint them, cut their hair, add big vulgar earrings just like when you were a kid. Then reenact your favorite scenes from *All About Eve* and *Night of the Living Dead*. There is something about an all-blue Barbie with red eyes that is beyond scary.

ANOTHER OPTION: Decorate the fingers of an old pair of mittens with yarn and fabric scraps and fabric paint.

SOURCES

Thrift stores are packed with wacky ingredients and fun objects. Most communities have the biggies, the Goodwill, Salvation Army, and St. Vincent DePaul. Also look for smaller shops benefiting community charities such as senior centers and humane societies. Many churches also have shops or regularly scheduled rummage sales. Look in the Yellow Pages under thrift shops, secondhand shops, and consignment shops. Browse garage sales, junk shops, and flea markets (not to be confused with expensive vintage shops and antique stores). And don't forget your own backyard! Excavate the closet, under the bed, Granny's attic, and your parents' basement, not to mention your recycling bin.

Visit your grocery store and favorite restaurant for potato sacks, rice sacks, and olive oil tins. Also try import specialty shops (not the expensive, fakey mega-import marts). Head downtown for the real thing: Italian, Indian, French, Chinese, Japanese, Vietnamese, and Indian groceries, delis, and specialty stores.

Look for images at shops that sell old magazines and books, and at stationery stores. Make color copies out of books from the library. Most libraries have old bound copies of *Life, Vogue,* etc.

Archie McPhee Catalog, the purveyors of tons of little plastic stuff, is only a phone call away. The catalog is worth getting if only to read the hilarious copy. Send your request to P.O. Box 30852, Seattle, WA 98103, or call 425-745-0711 for information and ordering.

ART SUPPLIES BY MAIL

Pearl Paint, 308 Canal Street, New York, NY 10013, 1-800-451-7327,
        1-800-732-7591 (fax)
Daniel Smith Co., 4150 1st Avenue South, Seattle, WA 98124, 1-800-426-6740
Utrecht, 33 35th Street, Brooklyn, NY 11232, 1-800-223-9132
Flax Art & Design, 1699 Market Street, San Francisco, CA 94103,
        1-800-547-7778

READING MATERIAL

Thrift Score, by Al Hoff, Harper Collins. Al also writes a great zine of the
        same name all about thrifting.
Cheap Date, a British zine on secondhand shopping with a few craft ideas.
Craphound, a zine featuring thousands of collected images, usable for
        personal projects.
Rubbery Whammy, a rubber-stamp zine from Britain featuring images of
        all the great stamps you can order.

These and many other zines can be found and ordered from Reading Frenzy,
921 SW Oak Street, Portland, OR 97205, 503-274-1449, www.readingfrenzy.com.
Or go to the library and look up books about folk art. There are many
beautifully photographed art books documenting various cultural traditions
from Mexico to Russia to inspire you and give you a dose of history.